All-in-One Meals

contents

Creamy Chicken Florentine

Makes 4 servings

PREP TIME
15 minutes

BAKE TIME
40 minutes

STAND TIME
5 minutes

1 can (10¾ ounces) Campbell's® Condensed Cream of Chicken Soup (Regular *or* 98% Fat Free)

1½ cups water

½ of a 20-ounce bag frozen cut leaf spinach, thawed and well drained (about 3½ cups)

1 can (about 14.5 ounces) Italian-style diced tomatoes

1 pound skinless, boneless chicken breasts, cut into 1-inch cubes

2½ cups *uncooked* penne pasta

½ cup shredded mozzarella cheese

1. Heat the oven to 375°F. Stir the soup, water, spinach, tomatoes and chicken in a 3-quart shallow baking dish. Cover the baking dish.

2. Bake for 20 minutes. Cook the pasta according to the package directions and drain well in a colander. Uncover the baking dish and stir in the pasta.

3. Bake for 20 minutes or until the pasta mixture is hot and bubbling. Sprinkle with the cheese. Let stand for 5 minutes or until the cheese is melted.

Chicken & Roasted Garlic Risotto

Makes 6 servings

PREP TIME
5 minutes

BAKE TIME
40 minutes

STAND TIME
5 minutes

1 can (10¾ ounces) Campbell's® Condensed Cream of Chicken Soup (Regular *or* 98% Fat Free)

1 can (10¾ ounces) Campbell's® Condensed Cream of Mushroom with Roasted Garlic Soup

2 cups water

1 package (10 ounces) frozen peas and carrots (about 2 cups)

1 cup *uncooked* regular long-grain white rice

6 skinless, boneless chicken breast halves

¼ cup grated Parmesan cheese

1. Stir the soups, water, vegetables and rice in a 13×9×2-inch (3-quart) shallow baking dish. Top with the chicken. **Cover.**

2. Bake at 375°F. for 40 minutes or until the chicken is cooked through. Sprinkle with the cheese. Let stand for 5 minutes.

Kitchen Tip

Traditionally, risotto is made by sautéing rice in butter then stirring broth into the rice a little at a time—very labor-intensive. This dish gives you the same creamy texture with a lot less work!

Chicken & Vegetable Bake

Makes 4 servings

PREP TIME
20 minutes

BAKE TIME
30 minutes

1 can (10¾ ounces) Campbell's® Condensed Cream of Celery Soup (Regular *or* 98% Fat Free)

½ cup milk

Dash ground black pepper

1 cup cooked broccoli *or* cauliflower florets

1 cup cooked sliced carrots

1 cup cooked cut green beans

¼ cup cooked red pepper strips

1 can (12.5 ounces) Swanson® Premium White Chunk Chicken Breast in Water, drained

1 can (2.8 ounces) French fried onions (1⅓ cups)

1. Stir the soup, milk, black pepper, broccoli, carrots, green beans, red pepper, chicken and ½ **can** onions in a 1½-quart casserole.

2. Bake at 350°F. for 20 minutes or until the chicken mixture is hot and bubbling. Stir the chicken mixture. Sprinkle with the remaining onions.

3. Bake for 10 minutes or until the onions are golden brown.

Easy Chicken Pot Pie

Makes 4 servings

PREP TIME
10 minutes

BAKE TIME
30 minutes

1 can (10¾ ounces) Campbell's® Condensed Cream of Chicken Soup (Regular *or* 98% Fat Free)

1 package (about 9 ounces) frozen mixed vegetables, thawed

1 cup cubed cooked chicken *or* turkey

½ cup milk

1 egg

1 cup all-purpose baking mix

Kitchen Tip

You can easily substitute Campbell's® Condensed Cream of Chicken with Herbs Soup for the Cream of Chicken.

1. Heat the oven to 400°F. Stir the soup, vegetables and chicken in a 9-inch pie plate.

2. Stir the milk, egg and baking mix in a small bowl. Spread the batter over the chicken mixture.

3. Bake for 30 minutes or until the topping is golden brown.

Herb Roasted Chicken & Vegetables

Makes 4 servings

PREP TIME
10 minutes

BAKE TIME
50 minutes

1 can (10 ¾ ounces) Campbell's® Condensed Cream of Mushroom Soup (Regular *or* 98% Fat Free)

⅓ cup water

2 teaspoons dried oregano leaves, crushed

4 medium potatoes, cut into quarters (about 1¼ pounds)

2 cups fresh *or* frozen baby carrots

4 bone-in chicken breast halves

½ teaspoon paprika

Kitchen **Tip**

Substitute white wine for the water.

1. Stir the soup, water, **1 teaspoon** of the oregano, potatoes and carrots in a roasting pan.

2. Top with the chicken. Sprinkle with the remaining oregano and paprika.

3. Bake at 400°F. for 50 minutes or until the chicken is cooked through. Stir the vegetable mixture before serving.

Baked Chicken & Cheese Risotto

Makes 4 servings

PREP TIME
10 minutes

BAKE TIME
45 minutes

STAND TIME
5 minutes

1 can (10¾ ounces) Campbell's® Condensed Cream of Mushroom Soup (Regular *or* 98% Fat Free)

1¼ cups water

½ cup milk

¼ cup shredded part-skim mozzarella cheese

3 tablespoons grated Parmesan cheese

1½ cups frozen mixed vegetables

2 skinless, boneless chicken breast halves (about ½ pound), cut into cubes

¾ cup *uncooked* Arborio *or* regular long-grain white rice

1. Stir the soup, water, milk, mozzarella cheese, Parmesan cheese, vegetables, chicken and rice in a 3-quart shallow baking dish. Cover the baking dish.

2. Bake at 400°F. for 35 minutes. Stir the rice mixture. Cover the baking dish.

3. Bake for 10 minutes or until the chicken is cooked through and the rice is tender. Let stand, covered, for 5 minutes.

Ham Asparagus Gratin

Makes 4 servings

PREP TIME
20 minutes

BAKE TIME
30 minutes

1 can (10¾ ounces) Campbell's® Condensed Cream of Asparagus Soup

½ cup milk

¼ teaspoon onion powder

¼ teaspoon ground black pepper

1½ cups cooked cut asparagus

1½ cups cubed cooked ham

2¼ cups corkscrew-shaped pasta (rotini), cooked and drained

1 cup shredded Cheddar cheese *or* Swiss cheese

1. Stir the soup, milk, onion powder, black pepper, asparagus, ham, pasta and **½ cup** cheese in a 2-quart shallow baking dish.

2. Bake at 400°F. for 25 minutes or until the ham mixture is hot and bubbling. Stir the ham mixture. Sprinkle with the remaining cheese.

3. Bake for 5 minutes or until the cheese is melted.

Zucchini, Chicken & Rice Casserole

Makes 4 servings

PREP TIME
15 minutes

BAKE TIME
35 minutes

STAND TIME
10 minutes

Vegetable cooking spray

1 package (12 ounces) refrigerated *or* thawed frozen breaded cooked chicken tenders, cut into bite-sized strips

2 large zucchini, cut in half lengthwise and thinly sliced (about 4 cups)

1 jar (7 ounces) whole roasted sweet peppers, drained and thinly sliced

1 cup *uncooked* quick-cooking brown rice

1 can (10¾ ounces) Campbell's® Condensed Cream of Celery Soup (Regular *or* 98% Fat Free)

1 soup can water

½ cup sour cream

Kitchen Tip

Choose zucchini that have firm, dark green skin.

1. Heat the oven to 375°F. Spray a 3-quart shallow baking dish with the cooking spray.

2. Stir the chicken, zucchini, peppers and rice in the baking dish.

3. Stir the soup, water and sour cream in a small bowl. Pour the soup mixture over the chicken mixture. Cover the baking dish.

4. Bake for 35 minutes or until the rice is tender. Let stand for 10 minutes. Stir the rice before serving.

Easy Chicken & Biscuits

Makes 4 servings

PREP TIME
10 minutes

BAKE TIME
35 minutes

1 can (10¾ ounces) Campbell's® Condensed Cream of Broccoli Soup (Regular *or* 98% Fat Free)

1 can (10¾ ounces) Campbell's® Condensed Cream of Potato Soup

⅔ cup milk

½ teaspoon poultry seasoning

⅛ teaspoon ground black pepper

2 cups frozen mixed vegetables

2 cups cubed cooked chicken *or* turkey

1 package (7.5 ounces) refrigerated biscuits

Kitchen **Tip**

Substitute Campbell's® Condensed Cream of Celery Soup for the Cream of Broccoli.

1. Stir the soups, milk, poultry seasoning, black pepper, vegetables and chicken in a 2-quart shallow baking dish.

2. Bake at 400°F. for 20 minutes or until the chicken mixture is hot and bubbling. Stir the chicken mixture. Top with the biscuits.

3. Bake for 15 minutes or until the biscuits are golden brown.

Chicken Broccoli Divan

Makes 4 servings

PREP TIME
15 minutes

BAKE TIME
20 minutes

1 pound fresh broccoli, cut into spears *or* 1 package (10 ounces) frozen broccoli spears, cooked and drained

1 can (12.5 ounces) Swanson® Premium White Chunk Chicken Breast in Water, drained

1 can (10¾ ounces) Campbell's® Condensed Broccoli Cheese Soup (Regular *or* 98% Fat Free)

⅓ cup milk

½ cup shredded Cheddar cheese

2 tablespoons dry bread crumbs

1 tablespoon butter, melted

Kitchen **Tip**

For cornflake topping, substitute cornflakes for the bread crumbs and omit the butter.

1. Place the broccoli and chicken into a 9-inch pie plate. Stir the soup and milk in a small bowl. Pour the soup mixture over the broccoli and chicken.

2. Sprinkle the cheese over the soup mixture. Stir the bread crumbs and butter in a small bowl. Sprinkle the bread crumb mixture over the cheese.

3. Bake at 450°F. for 20 minutes or until the cheese is melted and the bread crumb mixture is golden brown.

Turkey and Stuffing Casserole

Makes 6 servings

PREP TIME
15 minutes

BAKE TIME
25 minutes

Vegetable cooking spray

1 can (10¾ ounces) Campbell's® Condensed Cream of Mushroom Soup (Regular *or* 98% Fat Free)

1 cup milk *or* water

1 bag (16 ounces) frozen vegetable combination (broccoli, cauliflower, carrots), thawed

2 cups cubed cooked turkey *or* chicken

4 cups Pepperidge Farm® Herb Seasoned Stuffing

1 cup shredded Swiss *or* Cheddar cheese (about 4 ounces)

Kitchen Tip

*Substitute **3** cans (4.5 ounces each) Swanson® Premium White Chunk Chicken Breast in Water, drained, for the cubed cooked turkey.*

1. Heat the oven to 400°F. Spray a 2-quart casserole with the cooking spray.

2. Stir the soup and milk in a large bowl. Add the vegetables, turkey and stuffing and mix lightly. Spoon the turkey mixture into the casserole.

3. Bake for 20 minutes or until the turkey mixture is hot and bubbling. Stir the turkey mixture. Top with the cheese.

4. Bake for 5 minutes or until the cheese is melted.

Broccoli Fish Bake

Makes 4 servings

PREP TIME
15 minutes

BAKE TIME
20 minutes

1 package (about 10 ounces) frozen broccoli spears, cooked and drained

4 fresh *or* thawed frozen firm white fish fillets (cod, haddock *or* halibut) (about 1 pound)

1 can (10¾ ounces) Campbell's® Condensed Cream of Broccoli Soup

⅓ cup milk

¼ cup shredded Cheddar cheese

2 tablespoons dry bread crumbs

1 teaspoon butter, melted

⅛ teaspoon paprika

Kitchen **Tip**

You can substitute **1 pound** *fresh broccoli spears, cooked and drained, for the frozen.*

1. Place the broccoli into a 2-quart shallow baking dish. Top with the fish. Stir the soup and milk in a small bowl. Pour the soup mixture over the fish. Sprinkle with the cheese.

2. Stir the bread crumbs, butter and paprika in a small bowl. Sprinkle the crumb mixture over all.

3. Bake at 450°F. for 20 minutes or until the fish flakes easily when tested with a fork.

Country Turkey Casserole

Makes 5 servings

PREP TIME
10 minutes

BAKE TIME
25 minutes

1 can (10¾ ounces) Campbell's® Condensed Cream
   of Celery Soup (Regular *or* 98% Fat Free)
1 can (10¾ ounces) Campbell's® Condensed Cream
   of Potato Soup
1 cup milk
¼ teaspoon dried thyme leaves, crushed
⅛ teaspoon ground black pepper
4 cups cooked cut-up vegetables*
2 cups cubed cooked turkey *or* chicken
4 cups prepared Pepperidge Farm® Herb Seasoned
   Stuffing

*Use a combination of cut green beans **and** sliced carrots.*

1. Stir the soups, milk, thyme, black pepper, vegetables
and turkey in a 3-quart shallow baking dish. Spoon the
stuffing over the turkey mixture.

2. Bake at 400°F. for 25 minutes or until the stuffing
is golden brown.

Easy Beef & Pasta

Makes 4 servings

PREP TIME
5 minutes

COOK TIME
20 minutes

1 tablespoon vegetable oil

1 pound boneless beef sirloin steak, ¾-inch thick, cut into very thin strips

1 can (10¾ ounces) Campbell's® Condensed Tomato Soup (Regular *or* Healthy Request®)

½ cup water

1 bag (about 16 ounces) frozen vegetable pasta blend

1. Heat the oil in a 10-inch skillet over medium-high heat. Add the beef and cook until it's well browned, stirring often. Pour off any fat.

2. Stir the soup, water and vegetable pasta blend in the skillet and heat to a boil. Reduce the heat to low. Cover and cook for 5 minutes or until the beef is cooked through.